Vegan Keto

The vegan ketogenic diet cookbook
The ketogenic diet complete with
whole plant foods. Tasty recipes low
carb recipes to feed your mind and
promote weight loss naturally.

Table of Contents

This is a legally binding declaration that is considered both valid and fair by both the Committee of Publishers Association and the American Bar Association and should be considered as legally binding within the United States.

Furthermore, the information that can be found within the pages described forthwith shall be considered both accurate and truthful when it comes to freely available information and general consent. As such, any use, correct or incorrect, of the provided information will render the Publisher free of responsibility as to the actions taken outside of their direct purview. Regardless, there are zero scenarios where the original author or the Publisher can be deemed liable in any fashion for any damages or hardships that may result from any of the information discussed within.

Finally, any of the content found within is ultimately intended for entertainment purposes and should be thought of and acted on as such. Due to its inherently ephemeral nature, nothing discussed within should be taken as an assurance of quality, even when the words and deeds described herein indicated otherwise. Trademarks and copyrights mentioned within are done for informational purposes in line with fair use and should not be seen as an endorsement from the copyright or trademark holder.

Introduction

Congratulations on buying *Vegan Keto* and thank you for doing so.

There is an increasing interest in alternative diets for multiple reasons - health benefits, celebrities boasting about their diets on social media, people with dietary restrictions, moral or ethical reasons, etc., but this book will focus specifically on the vegan keto diet and all of its benefits.

We will start by discussing what both the vegan and keto diet are separately, so that we have laid a solid foundation to start from. By discussing what you could end up lacking with just the vegan diet, you will be able to decide if vegan keto is the right diet for you.

Next, we will move on to the benefits you will receive from combining both the vegan and keto diets together and what you can and cannot eat. With that out of the way, we will discuss kitchen equipment that is incredibly useful in making your transition to this diet as easy as possible, along with a seven-day meal plan to get you started. There is even a section on snacks and desserts for those with a sweet tooth.

By using the knowledge, tools, and skills that *Vegan Keto* will teach you, you will be able to implement this diet into your life as easily and seamlessly as possible.

There are plenty of books on this subject on the market, so thanks again for choosing this one! Every effort was made to ensure it is full of as much useful information as possible. Please enjoy!

Chapter 3: The Vegan Keto Diet

Having read both diets above, you may be wondering how it is possible to combine both of these diets together. The answer is probably simpler than you thought. By relying on plant-based foods that are high in fat, i.e. nuts, avocados, seeds, and coconut oil, vegan keto dieters are able to reach ketosis, too. In short, the only difference between the keto diet and the vegan keto diet is the exclusion of animal products. Vegan keto dieters still follow a high-fat, low-carb, moderate-protein diet. A few high-fat foods to incorporate are:

- Olive, nut, MCT, avocado, and coconut oil

- Cashew cheese

- Coconut yogurt

- Full-fat coconut milk/ cream

- Peanut, sunflower, almond, and cashew butter

Since both of these diets separately have certain health benefits, i.e. lower risk for heart disease and high blood pressure, easier weight loss that lowers the risk of type 2 diabetes, and better blood sugar levels, vegan keto dieters can reap all those benefits in one diet. It should be noted that ketogenic diets do rule out vegan staples like legumes and whole grains, but with careful planning, a vegan keto diet can be followed.

As with any restrictive diet, it is important that you supplement any vitamins, nutrients, and proteins that could be lacking from cutting entire food groups out of your diet. As we already discussed with vegan diets, the vegan keto diet can also cause deficiencies in vitamins D, B12, K2, calcium, iron, and zinc, along with lower omega-3-fats.

The same rules apply to this diet as they did with the vegan diets:

- Supplement needed vitamins and minerals

- Choose foods enriched with things like calcium and B12

- Whole-food focused

As with a keto diet, you are going to be changing what your body uses for energy, meaning you're going to face the same challenges (keto flu), recapped below:

- Nausea

- Less hunger

- Less energy

- Digestive difficulties (i.e. constipation or diarrhea

- Fogginess both mentally and physically

- Less endurance and strength

- Mild dehydration

- Changes in mouth and body odor

- Difficulty sleeping

- Dry mouth

- Muscle cramps

- Irritability

- Dizziness

The same coping mechanisms mentioned earlier will be helpful in managing the challenges listed above. To recap:

- Supplement with sodium, magnesium, and potassium

- Eat plenty of fiber-rich food

- Light physical activity

You will likely have read many of these foods to avoid in the chapters above, but below you will find a cohesive list of foods to avoid in order to follow the vegan keto diet:

- Meat, seafood, poultry, and fish

- Eggs

- Dairy

- Ingredients that are animal-based, i.e. honey, lactose, and whey protein

- Sweetener

- Whole grains

- Fruit (excluding berries)

- Products marketed as 'low-fat'

- Processed foods

- Legumes

- Soda, sweet tea, and other sugary drinks

- Vegetables high in starch

Since the vegan keto diet focuses on high-fat, low-carb foods, this diet does have its differences from a purely vegan diet. Because keto dieters get most of their protein and fat from animals and their byproducts, it is important to know what foods can help ensure you are receiving all the nutrients your body needs. This list is as follows:

- Avocados

- Nuts, nut butter, seeds, and seed butter

- Full-fat plant-based dairy (can be enriched with calcium)

- Healthy oils, i.e. MCT, avocado, and olive oil

- Berries

- Full-fat tempeh and tofu

- Vegetables without starch

- Condiments, i.e. lemon juice, pepper, salt, fresh herbs, spices without additives, and nutritional yeast

Since the vegan keto diet restricts or completely excludes many foods, it is possible that athletes, pregnant/ breastfeeding women, people with type 1 diabetes, or people with eating disorders may find this diet does not work for them. Below you will find a few common vegan cooking techniques, so you do not accidentally turn something that was originally vegan keto friendly, into something that is not.

- Broth/ Water Sautéing: Because a lot of oils are off-limits, being able to broth sauté is useful. You can use either vegetable broth or water, heat that in a pan, and then put your vegetables into that. You can also keep adding bit by bit as it is used so that the vegetables will caramelize like they would with oil.

- Instant Cooking: A safer, faster alternative to a stovetop pressure cooker is an instant pot. You simply put your food, i.e. stew, into the instant pot, set a timer, and let it do its thing.

- Stir-Frying: Using a wok is ideal, but you can manage with a big sauté pan. Different vegetables and plant-based noodles go into the pan with either a vegan keto approved oil or the above broth sautéing method and sauce.

- Slow Cooking: This is the opposite of instant cooking, but still has its perks. Slow cookers are ideal for those who would like to throw things into the slow cooker before work, and at the end of the day come home to a finished meal.

- Steaming: If you have got a steamer basket, you can easily steam fresh, crisp steamed vegetables.

- Roasting: Just like meat, vegetables can be roasted too - with or without oil.

Common Mistakes

It is easy to forget about certain minerals and vitamins that your body needs to function well, so keeping an eye on your intake (and possibly taking supplements as we discussed with vegan diets). The same rules apply here, and the same deficiencies apply as well – so watch out for them too!

It is also common to assume that all foods that are vegan are healthier. This is definitely not the case. There are countless vegan keto-friendly foods that are highly processed, high in sugar, and just generally not so great for you. They are things that you would want to eat in moderation. Do not make the mistake of trying to base your diet on processed foods. Instead, you should focus on whole foods, as mentioned previously.

Cutting out entire food groups can lead people to consume too few calories, so make sure that you are not just removing foods, but replacing them with vegan keto alternatives. Since your body needs a particular number of calories to function, making sure you are getting enough calories in your diet is vital.

Not drinking enough water is also a common mistake, but it is important in healthy, efficient digestion. If you are unable to flush out all the fiber you are consuming, you will likely end up with constipation and bloating.

Cons to Consider

All of the cons in both vegan and ketogenic diets also apply to the vegan keto diet. To quickly recap:

- People who lead a very active like will likely be unable to work with this diet.

- All of the symptoms of keto flu are still going to happen.

- Ketogenic diets are recommended to be followed under doctor supervision in a medical setting for specific health conditions. The risks associated with keto diets and ketosis do still apply to vegan keto diets.

- You run the risk of being deficient in certain proteins, minerals, and vitamins, which can lead to other health problems.

- Those with osteoporosis or diabetes should consult their general practitioner before starting a vegan keto diet.

- Eating out is going to be difficult.

Tips to Succeed

Every diet has its challenges, but having a few things to turn to can save the day, especially when things are getting rough. These are a few tips that can help you succeed:

- Do not get stuck on small problems and look at the big picture. Just by cutting out big food groups like meat and dairy, you can drastically improve your health. If you were eating fast food and takeout a few weeks ago, it is not the best idea to focus too heavily on only eating organic, local, fresh food. Start small and work your way up.

- Calling ahead or looking at online menus can make going out to eat way easier. You will not have to ask waiters what is in something and you can make sure you still get something you like.

- Do not limit yourself. Vegan diets are all about trying new things and moving from your comfort zone.

Do not forget that regular exercise is key in any diet.

Chapter 4: Cooking Vegan at Home

Alright, so you have made it this far! Now it is time to get cooking. We will cover everything from prepping, preparing, portioning, and even how your body's going to feel over the first seven days of the vegan keto diet. In the following pages you will find a seven-day meal plan, breakfast, lunch, dinner, dessert, and snacks included. You will learn what kitchen gadgets come in handy for certain recipes, and it is likely you will find a new favorite food. Before we jump into the seven-day meal plan, it is important that we cover a few basics that will likely apply to most of the recipes you will learn below.

Most meals should always start with prepping because you will likely have to cut, dice, or mince several fruits or vegetables. It is better to cut more than you need than too little because the last thing you want is to try to cut broccoli for your stir-fry after everything is already cooking. Even if you cut too much of something, you can store it in the fridge for a few days and use it for something else. This is where glass storage dishes come in handy! Do not forget, part of the prep is making sure all your knives are sharp and ready to go.

Day One

Breakfast: Low-Carb Maple Oatmeal

Cook time: 20 to 30 minutes

Servings: 4

Calories: 374

Fat: 34.59 grams

Protein: 9.25 grams

Net Carbs: 12.37 grams

Kitchen tools you will need:

- Food processor or blender

- Large pot

- Measuring spoons/ cups

Ingredients:

- Chia seeds

- Walnuts and pecans

- Sunflower seeds

- Blackberries/ strawberries

Steps:

- Start by making low-carb oatmeal using chia seeds. Put sunflower seeds, pecans, and walnuts into a food processor until crumbled.

- In a big pot, add all three ingredients and chia seeds and simmer on low for 20 to 30 minutes, stirring until oatmeal is thick.

- Remove from stove.

- Use whichever milk you prefer, i.e. coconut, almond, or cashew.

- Top with fresh fruit or additional nuts.

- Serve.

Lunch: Zucchini Noodles with Avocado Sauce

Cook time: 10 minutes

Servings: 2

Calories: 313

Fat: 26.8 grams

Protein: 6.8 grams

Net Carbs: 18.7 grams

Kitchen tools you will need:

- Spiralizer or peeler

- Measuring spoons/ cups

- Blender or food processor

- Large bowl

- Sauté pan

Ingredients:

- Walnuts or pine nuts: 4 tablespoons

- Lemon juice: 2 teaspoons

- Avocado: 1

- Basil or spinach: 1 ¼ cups

- Water: 1/3 cup

- Zucchini: 1

Steps:

- Slice off one end of your zucchini and place your spiralizer against the flat surface, cranking the handle to make your noodles.

- Using either broth sauté or a vegan keto accepted oil, cook zucchini over medium heat for 1 minute.

- Add water; cook until zucchini is at the desired softness, 5 to 7 minutes.

- Blend avocado, basil or spinach, lemon juice, and walnuts or pine nuts until texture is smooth.

- Place both the sauce and noodles into a large bowl and mix.

- Top with cherry tomatoes.

- Serve.

Dinner: Fresh Basil Bell Pepper Pizza

Cook time: 25 to 35 minutes

Servings: 1 pizza

Calories: 410

Fat: 27.7 grams

Protein: 20.22 grams

Net Carbs: 6.46 grams

Kitchen tools you will need:

- Measuring spoons/ cups

- Cheese grater (optional)

- Mixing bowl

- Rolling pin

- Baking sheet

Ingredients:

- Lukewarm water: 1 cup

- Ground psyllium husk: 2 tablespoons

- Coconut flour: 2/4 cup

- Vegan keto approved oil: 1 tablespoon

- Salt: ¼ teaspoon

- Basil: to taste

- Peppers: to taste

- Grated vegan cheese: to taste

Steps:

- Add salt, psyllium husk, coconut flour, your preferred oil, and water to a big mixing bowl.

- Mix with a wooden spoon or spatula to start, and then use your hands to work the dough for 1 minute. You want the dough to dry as you knead.

- Make a ball with the dough; place it back in the mixing bowl for 10 minutes at room temperature.

- When the dough is firm, add your choice of oil to parchment paper and place the dough on top. Using your hands, flatten the ball, place another sheet of parchment paper over the dough, and begin rolling it out with your rolling pin. If you do not use the parchment paper, the dough will get stuck to your rolling pin.

- Flatten to desired thickness. If you prefer crispy pizza, roll your dough thinner.

- Remove the top layer of parchment paper and place the pizza (with the parchment paper under it) onto a baking sheet and pre-bake at 430 degrees Fahrenheit for 12 to 15 minutes.

- Remove from oven.

- Top with fresh tomato sauce, vegan shredded cheese, peppers, and basil to taste.

- Place the pizza back into the oven for 5 to 8 minutes, whenever your cheese has fully melted.

- Serve.

Day Two

Breakfast: Keto Vegan Scramble

Cook time: 10 to 15 minutes

Servings: 5

Calories: 21.4

Fat: 17.56 grams

Protein: 10.09 grams

Net Carbs: 4.74 grams

Kitchen tools you will need:

- Tofu press (optional)

- Skillet

- Potato masher (optional)

- Measuring cups/ spoons

Ingredients:

- Vegan cheddar cheese: 3 ounces

- Baby spinach: 1 cup

- Grape tomatoes: 3

- Salt: ½ teaspoon

- Garlic powder: ½ teaspoon

- Turmeric: ½ teaspoon

- Avocado oil: 3 tablespoons

- Nutritional yeast: 1 ½ tablespoon

- Firm tofu: 14 ounces

- Diced yellow onion: 2 tablespoons

Steps:

- Place your tofu into a tofu press; after pressing most of the water out, put it aside.

- Dice 3 grape tomatoes.

- Heat 1/3 avocado oil over medium heat in a skillet and add the onion.

- Cook until onions are translucent and soft.

- Add the block of tofu to the pan, crumble with fork or potato masher, until consistency resembles scrambled eggs.
- Use the rest of the avocado oil over the top, add garlic powder, salt, nutritional yeast, and turmeric; stir.
- Continue cooking over medium heat, occasionally stirring until the liquid is gone.
- Add in tomatoes, baby spinach, and vegan cheese.
- Cook until cheese has melted.
- Serve.

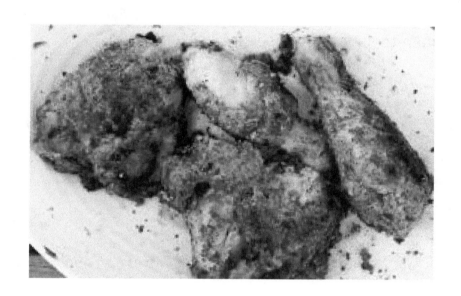

Lunch: Spiralized Cucumber Salad with Wasabi Cucumber Avocado Dressing

Cook time: 20 minutes

Servings: 4

Kitchen tools you will need:

- Chef's knife

- Measuring spoons/ cups

- Blender, immersion blender, or food processor

- Spiralizer or vegetable peeler

Ingredients:

- Avocado oil: 2 tablespoons

- Sea salt: ¼ teaspoon

- Garlic powder: ½ teaspoon

- Wasabi powder: 2 tablespoons

- Rice vinegar: 2 teaspoons

- Green onion stalks: 2 to 4

- Chopped cucumber: 1/3 cup

- Avocado: 1

- Lime juice: ½ lime

- Shredded carrot: ½ cup or to taste

- English cucumber: 1

- Toasted sesame seeds: 1 to 2 teaspoons

- Greens (spinach, kale, lettuce, arugula): 3 to 4 cups

Steps:

- Place avocado, cucumber, lime juice, wasabi powder, garlic powder, sea salt, rice vinegar, avocado oil, and green onion into a blender or food processor.

- For a creamier dressing, use an immersion blender.

- Adjust seasoning to taste.

- Cut both ends off the English cucumber, and use a spiralizer to craft easy noodles.

- Shred carrots.

- Place greens of choice in a large bowl, add cucumbers, sesame seeds, and shredded carrots; finish with cucumber avocado dressing.

- Serve.

Dinner: Spicy Curry Thai Cauliflower Soup

Cook time: 35 to 45 minutes

Servings: 6

Kitchen tools you will need:

- Baking tray

- Blender or food processor

- Large pot

- Chef's knife/ paring knife

Ingredients:

- Sliced green onions: to taste

- Diced yellow onion: 1

- Cauliflower: 1

- Lemon zest: 1

- Vegetable broth: 1 quart

- Unsweetened coconut milk: 14 ounces

- Vegan keto hot sauce of your choice

- Coconut oil: 2 tablespoons

- Sea salt and pepper: to taste

- Thai red curry paste: 4 tablespoons

Steps:

- Slice onion into quarters and cut cauliflower; place on baking tray lined with parchment paper.

- Top with pepper, salt, and avocado oil; toss to mix.

- Bake at 400 degrees Fahrenheit for 20 minutes; let cool.

- Once cool, add to food processor or blender with vegetable broth, lemon zest, and red curry paste until smooth.

- In a pot over medium heat, add above ingredients and coconut milk; stir.

- Season with salt and pepper to taste, then bring to a simmer and leave for 10 to 15 minutes.
- Finish with green onions and hot sauce on top.
- Serve.

Day Three

Breakfast: <u>Vegan Pancakes</u>

Cook time: 10 to 12 minutes

Servings: 2

Kitchen tools you will need:

- Frying pan

- Small mixing bowl

- Ladle or large spoon

- Measuring cups/ spoons

Ingredients:

- Ground flax: 1 tablespoon

- Unsweetened almond butter: 2 tablespoons

- Baking powder: ½ teaspoon

- Unsweetened almond milk: ¼ cup

- Coconut flour: 1 tablespoon

- Liquid sweetener of your choice: to taste

- Preferred oil of choice, i.e. almond, sunflower, or avocado

Steps:

- Put your oil of choice in a frying pan over medium-low heat.

- Combine almond milk and almond butter in small bowl; do the same with baking powder, ground flax, and coconut flower.

- Mix dry and wet ingredients along with liquid sweetener of choice; let sit for 1 to 2 minutes.

- Once skillet is hot, use a ladle or large spoon to scoop the batter onto the pan; cook 4 to 5 minutes, then flip and cook an additional 2 to 3 minutes.

- Finish with berries, coconut cream and almonds to taste.
- Serve.

Lunch: Broccoli Fried Rice

Cook time: 8 to 13 minutes

Servings: 4

Calories: 87

Fat: 5 grams

Protein: 2 grams

Net Carbs: 7 grams

Kitchen tools you will need:

- Blender or food processor

- Skillet or sauté pan

- Measuring spoons/ cups

- Grater (optional)

Ingredients:

- Avocado oil: 1 tablespoon

- Riced broccoli: 4 cups (roughly 2 full heads)

- Finely minced garlic: 1 tablespoon

- Toasted sesame oil: 1.5 teaspoons

- Coconut aminos: 1 tablespoon

- Chopped bulb scallions: 2

- Chopped parsley: 4 tablespoons

- Grated frozen ginger: ¼ teaspoon

- Sea salt: ¼ to ½ teaspoon

Steps:

- Chop garlic and parsley

- Add broccoli to a food processor and blend until grain-sized.

- Add avocado oil to skillet over medium heat once hot.

- Put broccoli and garlic into the pan and sauté for 1 minute.

- Use sea salt, coconut aminos, and toasted sesame oil to season the rice to taste; additional

2 minutes of sautéing or until broccoli is bright green; turn off the stove.

- Grate ginger on top of the rice while warm and top with lime juice, parsley, and scallions.
- Serve.

© Spill the Spices

Dinner: Cauliflower Mushroom Burger with Crisp Avocado Fries

Cook time: 35 to 45 minutes

Servings: 6

Calories: 340

Fat: 25 grams

Protein: 9.7 grams

Net Carbs: 25.5 grams

Kitchen tools you will need:

- Chef's knife or paring knife

- Measuring spoons/ cups

- Baking sheet

- Skillet or sauté pan

- Mixing bowl

- Avocado cutter

- 2 small mixing bowls

Ingredients (Burger):

- Almond flour: 6 tablespoons

- Minced garlic: 1 clove

- Chopped yellow onion: ½

- Dried rosemary: ½ teaspoon

- Grated cauliflower: 2 cups (roughly ½ a head)

- Chopped mushrooms: 8 ounces

- Avocado oil: 1 tablespoon

- Salt and pepper: to taste

- Vegan barbeque sauce: to taste

- Lettuce/ greens

Ingredients (Fries):

- Almond milk (or your preferred vegan keto friendly milk): ¼ cup

- Avocado: 1

- Almond flour: ½ cup

- Pepper and salt: to taste

Steps:

- Place parchment paper on 2 baking sheets and set aside.

- Chop onion and place cauliflower in food processor until rice-consistency; mince garlic and chop mushrooms.

- In a sauté pan or skillet over medium heat, add avocado oil and onion; cook 2 minutes, then add garlic, mushrooms, and rosemary.

- Sauté for 3 to 4 minutes, then add riced cauliflower.

- Move to mixing bowl and let cool.

- Once cool, add almond flour and mix with a spoon until thicker, then use hands to form patties.

- Place on parchment-lined tray and cook at 400 degrees Fahrenheit for 30 minutes.
- If you have an avocado cutter you can use it to peel and pit, otherwise, use a paring knife; slice into strips resembling fries.
- Fill two small bowls, one with almond flour and the other with your chosen milk; dip avocado slices into milk to wet, then into the almond flower until evenly coated, and finished with salt and pepper.
- Place avocado strips on baking sheet; cook for 10 minutes at 425 degrees Fahrenheit; flip; continue for an additional 10 minutes.
- Use lettuce leaves for your bun; add burger, spinach, tomatoes, and whatever condiments you prefer – vegan ketchup and mustard are out there. Chipotle hummus goes great with avocado fries.
- Plate burger and fries; serve.

© YummyLummy.com

Day Four

Breakfast: Spaghetti Squash Tots

Cook time: 25 to 35 minutes

Servings: 6

Calories: 22

Fat: .4 grams

Protein: .5 grams

Net Carbs: 4.8 grams

Kitchen tools you will need:

- Paring knife or chef's knife

- Mini muffin pan

- Mixing bowl

Ingredients:

- Black pepper: ¼ teaspoon

- Sea salt/ kosher salt: to taste

- Avocado oil/ oil of choice

- Thinly sliced scallion: 1

- Spaghetti squash: 1

Steps:

- Use oil of choice to lightly grease a mini-muffin pan; set aside

- Poke several holes into spaghetti squash, then microwave for 7 to 8 minutes on high until lightly softened.

- Cut squash in half lengthwise; remove seeds; scrape out squash strands with a fork and toss the skins.

- Remove as much moisture from the squash as possible to get crispier tots, place in large bowl, and use a knife to cut the strands into smaller noodles.

- Toss in pepper, salt, and scallions; stir.

- With a spoon, fill each mini-muffin cup roughly halfway; flatten with fingers.

- Drizzle oil of choice sparingly over top of each mini-muffin; place in oven at 425 degrees Fahrenheit for approximately 10 minutes.

- Remove from oven and cool for 5 to 7 minutes.

- Finish with salt to taste.

- Serve.

Lunch: Almond Butter Shirataki Noodles

Cook time: 10 to 15 minutes

Servings: 1

Calories: 190

Protein: 8.1 grams

Net Carbs: 19.3 grams

Kitchen tools you will need:

- Large saucepan or wok

- Paring knife or chef's knife

- Measuring cups/ spoons

Ingredients:

- Almond butter: 1 tablespoon

- Coconut aminos: 2 tablespoons

- Chopped carrot: 1

- Shredded cabbage: ¼ of whole cabbage

- Diced spring onions: 3

- Minced garlic: 2 cloves

- Broccoli with long stems: 100 grams

- Coconut oil: 1 tablespoon

- Shirataki noodles (tofu noodles): 1 pack

- Optional – sriracha sauce: 1 to 2 teaspoons

Steps:

- Dice spring onions, mince garlic, shred cabbage, cut carrots, and chop broccoli.

- Heat coconut oil in a large saucepan or wok over medium heat; add onions and garlic; cook until soft (roughly 2 to 3 minutes).

- Add cabbage, broccoli, and carrots; stir-fry.

- While your vegetables cook, rinse Shirataki noodles well with warm water.

- Add noodles to wok or saucepan with the vegetables and cook for 7 to 10 minutes.

- 1 to 2 minutes before fully cooked add coconut aminos, almond butter, and sriracha (optional); stir to warm and create a sauce.

- Serve.

Dinner: Taco Skillet

Cook time: 25 to 30 minutes

Servings: 2

Calories: 215

Fat: 1 gram

Protein: 4 grams

Net Carbs: 15 grams

Kitchen tools you will need:

- Large pan

- Paring knife or chef's knife

- Measuring cups/ spoons

Ingredients:

- Water: ¼ cup

- Grapeseed oil: 2 tablespoons

- Vegan friendly taco seasoning: 2 tablespoons

- Diced walnuts: ½ cup

- Diced bell pepper: 1 (any color)

- Diced zucchini: 1

- Diced eggplant with skin: 1

- Diced tomatoes and green chilies: 8 ounces

Steps:

- Dice bell pepper, zucchini, walnuts, and eggplant; set aside.

- Heat grapeseed oil in large pan until lightly shimmering; add bell pepper over medium-high heat for 3 to 4 minutes until lightly browned.

- Add zucchini and eggplant; cook for 7 to 10 minutes until halfway reduced.

- Top with diced tomatoes, green chilies, and walnuts; stir and add taco seasoning with water.

- Continue cooking for 7 to 10 minutes or until water cooks off.

- Serve.

www.pinkwhen.com

Day Five

Breakfast: Coconut Milk Berry Chia Pudding

Cook time: 5 minutes

Servings: 4

Calories: 160.5

Fat: 8 grams

Protein: 4 grams

Net Carbs: 18 grams

Kitchen tools you will need:

- Blender or food processor
- Mixing bow
- Measuring cups/ spoons
- Spatula

Ingredients:

- Coconut milk: 3 cups

- Sweetener: to taste

- Chia seeds: 6 to 8 tablespoons

- MCT or coconut oil (optional): 1 to 2 tablespoons

- Vegan protein powder: 2 tablespoons

- Frozen or fresh berries: 2 cups

- Sea salt: 1 to 2 pinches

Cook time: 40 minutes or allow pudding to set overnight

- Mix your choice of frozen or fresh berries, coconut milk, MCT or coconut oil, vegan protein powder, 1 to 2 pinches of salt, and sweetener in a blender until smooth.

- Place chia seeds and blended coconut berry milk into mixing bowl; stir.

- Refrigerate overnight.

- Finish with a choice of toppings, i.e. strawberries, flakes of almond, and cacao powder.

- Serve.

Lunch: Blueberry, Almond, and Avocado Salad

Cook time: 2 to 4 minutes

Servings: 1

Calories: 256.4

Fat: 20.2 grams

Protein: 6.2 grams

Net Carbs: 4 grams

Kitchen tools you will need:

- Serving-sized bowl

- Avocado cutter or paring knife

- Measuring cups/ spoons

- Small side dish

Ingredients:

- Blueberries: 1 ounce

- Sliced almonds: 15 grams

- Avocado: ½

- Coconut or MCT oil: 1 tablespoon

- Spinach and kale mix: ½ cup

- Arugula mix: 1 cup

- Vegan balsamic vinaigrette: 1 to 2 tablespoons

Steps:

- Add spinach and arugula mix to a 1-serving-sized bowl.

- Use an avocado cutter or paring knife to cut and pit an avocado; slice to preferred size (refrigerate to save).

- Top salad with almonds and blueberries.

- In a small side dish, put vegan balsamic vinaigrette and coconut or MCT oil.

- Serve.

Dinner: Chipotle Lime Tacos

Cook time: 25 to 30 minutes

Servings: 6

Calories: 191

Fat: 11 grams

Protein: 1.4 grams

Net Carbs: 23 grams

Kitchen tools you will need:

- Mixing jar

Ingredients (taco seasoning):

- Cayenne: ¼ teaspoon

- Sea salt: 1 teaspoon

- Black pepper: 1 teaspoon

- Onion powder: 1 teaspoon

- Oregano: 1 teaspoon

- Granulated garlic: 2 teaspoons

- Smoked paprika: 1 tablespoon

- Cumin: 1 tablespoon

- Ground chipotle: 1 tablespoon

Ingredients (tacos):

- Vegan jackfruit carnitas (packaged): 1 pack

- Coconut oil: 1 tablespoon

- Vegan wraps: 6

- Cilantro: 1 bunch

- Guacamole: 1 cup

- Shredded lettuce: 2 cups

- Salsa of choice: ½ cup

- Onions: to taste

Steps:

- Mix together cayenne, black pepper, onion powder, oregano, sea salt, granulated garlic, cumin, ground chipotle, and smoked paprika; set aside.

- Over medium heat add coconut oil to pan; when oil is hot, add packaged jackfruit and spice mix.

- Cook for 7 to 10 minutes.

- In a clean skillet, heat wraps, 30 to 60 seconds per side.

- Top with shredded lettuce, onions, guacamole, and cilantro.

- Serve.

Day Six

Breakfast: <u>Avocado Raspberry Smoothie</u>

Cook time: 2 to 4 minutes

Servings: 2

Calories: 227

Fat: 20 grams

Protein: 2.5 grams

Net Carbs: 12.8 grams

Kitchen tools you will need:

- Food processor or blender

- Measuring cups/ spoons

- Avocado cutter/ paring knife

Ingredients:

- Unsweetened frozen raspberries: ½ cup

- Water: 1 1/3 cup

- Pitted and peeled avocado: 1

- Lemon juice: 3 tablespoons

- Liquid sugar of choice: 2 tablespoons

Steps:

- Use a paring knife to pit and peel 1 ripe avocado.

- Add liquid sugar of choice, lemon juice, water, avocado, and unsweetened frozen raspberries into a blender; mix until consistency is smooth.

Lunch: Cashew Scallion Cheese and Vegan Burger Salad

Cook time: 7 to 12 minutes

Servings: 1

Calories: 641.7

Fat: 43 grams

Protein: 42.2 grams

Net Carbs: 18 grams

Kitchen tools you will need:

- Food processor or blender

- Skillet or frying pan

- Avocado cutter (optional)

- Paring knife

- Measuring cups/ spoons

- Cutting board (bamboo or wood are preferred)

Ingredients (salad):

- Raw broccoli: ¼ cup

- Avocado: ½

- Apple cider vinegar: to taste

- Spinach and arugula mix: 3 cups

- MCT or avocado oil: 2 teaspoons

- Red cabbage: ¼ cup

- Sliced radishes: to taste

- Vegan burger patty of choice, i.e. Field Roast

Ingredients (cashew scallion cheese):

- Raw, pre-rinsed and soaked: 1 cup

- Raw sunflower seeds, unsalted: ½ cup

- Chopped celery: ¼ cup

- Nutritional yeast: 3 tablespoons

- Chopped scallions: ¼ cup (roughly 2 to 3)

- Sea salt: 1 teaspoon

- Fresh lemon juice: ¼ cup

Steps:

- Chop scallions (white and green parts), celery, broccoli, red cabbage, and radishes; use an avocado cutter or paring knife to pit and peel ½ an avocado; set aside.

- In a skillet or frying pan, heat your vegan burger; add salt and pepper to taste; cook for 3-5 minutes, flipping halfway through; cover and remove from heat.

- In a food processor, add scallions, raw cashews, celery, lemon juice, sea salt, unsalted sunflower seeds, and nutritional yeast; blend for 1 to 2 minutes.

- If the mixture is too thick, add 2 to 3 tablespoons of water; mix until the desired cheese-texture is achieved.

- In a bowl, add the spinach and arugula mixture, broccoli, red cabbage, and radishes topped with MCT or avocado oil and apple cider vinegar.

- Top off with cashew scallion cheese and a vegan burger.

- Serve.

Dinner: Coconut Curry Soup

Cook time: 10 to 15 minutes

Servings: 4

Calories: 425

Fat: 33 grams

Protein: 18 grams

Net Carbs: 19 grams

Kitchen tools you will need:

- Large pot

- Measuring spoons/ cups

- Paring knife

- Chopping board

- Tofu press (optional)

Ingredients:

- Melted coconut oil: 4 tablespoons

- Fresh chopped cilantro: ¼ cup

- Baby spinach: 1 cup

- Diced extra-firm tofu: 16 ounces

- Black pepper: to taste

- Sea salt: 1 teaspoon

- Liquid sugar of choice, i.e. stevia: 4 drops

- Unsweetened peanut butter: 2 tablespoons

- Vegan unflavored protein powder: 2 tablespoons

- Vegetable stock: 1 cup

- Diced zucchini: 1

- Diced carrot: 1

- Unsweetened coconut milk (full-fat): 1 ½ cups

- Vegan red curry paste: 2 ½ tablespoons

- Sliced garlic: 2 cloves

- Thin-sliced green bell pepper: ½

- Thin-sliced scallions: 2

- Vegan butter of choice: ¼ cup

Steps:

- Dice zucchini, carrot, garlic, green bell pepper, and scallions (keep green and white separate); set aside.

- Over medium-high heat in large pot melt vegan butter of choice; then add in scallion whites and green bell pepper; cook for 1 to 2 minutes.

- Add coconut milk, carrot, zucchini, vegan protein powder, vegetable stock, liquid sugar of choice, pepper, salt, and peanut butter; stir.

- Once boiling, lower to simmer for 7 to 10 minutes; if necessary, adjust seasoning.

- Use tofu press to remove water from tofu, cut to size, and then add to pot with cilantro and spinach; to warm, cook for 5 minutes.

- Either plate all 4 bowls or portion them out.

- Finish by melting 1 tablespoon coconut oil over top with cilantro and scallion greens to taste.

- Serve.

CPSIA information can be obtained
at www.ICGtesting.com
Printed in the USA
BVHW092147200421
605422BV00002B/86

9 781801 674164